POEMS FROM THE MIND OF I.R. ART

WINTERTIME CATERPILLAR

Life it's a poetic dance

By: Isaiah Robinson

DEDICATIONS

Dedicated: To my Grandmother,

Mother, Father, Brother & Sisters, and

My baby girl Jaida

CONTENT

STRENGTH	GLADIATOR
SYMBOLISM	UNBREAKABLE
IMAGINATION	CONSCIOUSNESS
ILLUMINATE	LIBERATE
HEALTH	CHAMPION
SACRIFICE	DEMONSTRATE
SUCCESS	ACCOMPLISH
DISCIPLINE	MILLIONS
WEALTH	MILLIONAIRE
PERSEVERANCE	ETERNITY
IMMACULATE	PERSISTENCE
INGENUITY	OPPORTUNITY
INSPIRATION	PREPARATION
POWER	ABUNDANCE
MOTIVATION	VISION
DETERMINATION	ASPIRATION
ACCOUNTABLE	AMBIENCE
DEDICATION	INTOXICATE
MOMENTUM	REVITALIZE
AMBITION	INVIGORATE
ELEVATE	INCLINATION
WARRIOR	NOURISHMENT

STRENGTH

Strength in hands, strength in eyes, strength in minds,

But there is no strength in lies,

The lies make the weak feel strength, when the weak feel strength,

They realize it was all lies, all the things I despise

My strength defines the electrolytes moving round in my mind,

My strength is truth, my strength is love, my strength is life

It takes no strength to take a life, it takes all strength to make a life,

Pain in my mind like fingernails being pulled,

My strength talks to me it tells me there is no pain,

Pain is my gain to measure my treasure,

I told the world it was my pleasure, my strength breaks down into my

pleasure, your weakness breaks down into your failure,

I try I try and I try again, I look around at my loneliest I can not find a

Friend, all I found was a Mercedes-Benz and some ends,

Prices you will have to pay for success takes strength,

Your strength will take patience, practice, and perseverance,

And just remember your strength is under surveillance like small

eyeballs watching fishbowls, but none of it matters as long as you reach

your goals.

SYMBOLISM

Pyramids lies in the eyes of many, street kids standing on corners for

Twenties, like greedy people at buffets looking for plenty,

I represent the tenacity of my audacity to symbolize someone great,

The symbolism of me is my faith,

It was told we were made in his image, So it's only right we replenish his

Image in our life and do what's right,

Empty bottles and crowded ashtrays the symbolism of failed dreams or

progress in motion, fell in love and stumbled like I took the wrong

potion, everything started off smooth like putting on lotion,

things quickly dried up, got rough, ran out of lotion,

pretty skies fireflies symbolize the remind of better days,

I remember the days where school grades represented the symbolism

of better ways, now hairs are all grey and better ways only come in

waves, and like California surfers you have to catch them,

a thousand eyeballs watching 500 T.V.'s,

the symbolism of thoughts destroyed and thoughts created,

people ask who made this, I stand and announce I created this,

let your life be a symbol for what you create, there's no time

waste when its time to be great.

IMAGINATION

No limitation on imagination, like spacewalker's lost in space,

This is infinity and beyond or beyond to infinity,

A classroom full of minds focused on future frustrations,

Problem solved,

No problem solved when no questions asked,

Questions are the hallways in the house of imagination,

Answers get you to the right door or left door,

Bad thoughts left my imagination sore, like toothaches from candy,

It started off as sweets but still ended badly,

Sadly I smile with missing teeth, but still shinning all pearly whites,

It was imagination of implantation that made these pearly whites shine,

In my mind is what's mines,

In my mind ideas are blind and gave to the world,

The world is just a templet for the mind imagination to reach elevation,

Leave your mark with motivation and inspiration,

A 1000 paintings and A 1000 books,

There holds the power to change a 1000 people faces and minds who

Look.

ILLUMINATE

This light shines and blinds like the fury and intensity of the sun,

You can hide, you can run, but this light is still going to come,

Illuminate the people like fresh knowledge in new minds,

Lightbulbs over heads cartoon version of a new idea,

There would be no light without the darkness, the darkness can't

escape the light, 200 watts of light in your life every day of your life,

it took all night to get this bright, you would be a fool if you think this

all happened overnight,

we had to vibrate to illuminate to get this right,

in one night light can be brought to a kid when parents reads them a

bedtime story, sunshine break threw clouds and make nice days and

bad times synonymous, you illuminate when you realize it's all the

same,

eyeballs won't look at you the same, but like moths they will be

attracted to your flame, they will say they understand your pain,

caution sign in the mind when I see the rain,

they say you can be a star, have fortune and fame,

my only question when will they forget my name.

HEALTH

Higher goals and plateaus for my mind, body and soul,

On the road paved with gold drinking a green smoothie,

Digest 100 books or 100 vegetables,

This is what consumes me, they say you are what you eat,

I eat what I consume like nourishment for babies in the womb,

Brand-new beautiful butterflies coming out their cocoon,

Young eyes old eyes looking at the same moon,

Doesn't matter who you are death is coming soon,

Better you live better then living the best fake life,

Wrong is wrong right is right, ignorance is still bliss,

Looking up at the sky thinking I don't understand this,

Looking inside myself I find all understanding,

I look long, I look far, I look wide,

The whole time the cure was my mind, mind over matter or do you

Think does your mind even matter,

I laugh then cry while climbing life's ladder,

Blood moving as fast as the world spin,

Coming back then coming back again.

SACRIFICE

Lonely talents, being great at something nobody wants to be good at,

Show respect and take off your hat, wipe your feet on the door mat,

When you look back do you see facts,

Lies help you meet your demise like flies 24 hour,

It started off sweet then ended up sour,

Like your favorite candy it taste better with no teeth,

More lies for your eyes, but what lies underneath,

The truth is better then before, it was better then I thought,

Sacrifice in the life of the one who thought twice,

It took 1 2 3 4 5 times and I didn't lose my mind,

Momentum made me count,

The second guess was the doubt,

Give everything you got like climbing a mountain,

Same feeling as kid playing in fountain,

Looking around for the horizon but I can't find one,

Hopes to see another one,

What was sacrificed doubts of seeing another one,

Then realize there was only one.

SUCCESS

A thousand dreams plotted on, planned out and accomplished,

A thousand people mad at what got demolished,

Life is more than one try, but just remember you only get one try,

A lot of blood, sweat, and cries,

Pain and joy living in the same eyes, husband & wife living the same

Life's at opposite times, try just one more time,

Fail just one more time, then try again,

Never thought about quitting like babies trying to walk,

It was bittersweet, then sweet turn to bitter,

As a dog looks at its litter, a man becomes a winner,

I think to myself what's for dinner, enjoy the fruits of your labor,

My labor bears fruit like those two trees in the Garden of Eden,

Sacrifices for success, looking around like what's next,

Everyone thinks there the best, but no one applied to take the test,

Unprepared fools missing opportunity, they say practice makes perfect,

Well this is perfect timing, like stars brightly shinning,

This was not coincidences, this was all calculated,

I don't care if 100 million people hate this,

It took forever to reach this greatness.

DISCIPLINE

Cruel punishment or precise strategy,

It was never easy to be your majesty, but I gladly try,

Sometimes effort can live forever, sometimes forever can be a little

better, what does it take to push threw get threw like pencil points

threw paper, product of bad decision or voluntary victim pick one,

a lot of closed doors but a lot of open windows,

innuendos to the soul, never forgetting the goals,

no one knows what you hold, everyone knows what you hold when you

fold, no poker face, you don't play poker so you felt no need

for a poker face, now I can see the pain on your face,

In this life you will face challenges, what's a life unchallenged,

How do we manage, discipline our self, selflove or self-hate,

One road to be great, one road to be fake,

No strategy for faith, meditate contemplate these are the things the

mind makes, last chance was no chance but got one more chance,

Stick to the script like Broadway performers,

Off script blooper, blame yourself blame your tutor,

You train you train your brain taught you everything, you taught your

Brain nothing, won't you teach your brain something.

WEALTH

Abundance in many as I look at plenty,

Wanting the ending to be predictable, my favorite movies,

Executed plans can feel like a movie,

Future generations benefiting from the fruit of past generation labor,

Be a good neighbor, value becomes me as I become great,

You fall, you crawl, just to get back to the top,

This momentum will never stop, brain popped, thinking to much,

Skip schools to use brain waves as tools, still consider a fool,

Family, friends, or foes, it's all fuel,

Imagination my destination to reach greatness, great is not the goal,

1000 tons of gold is the goal, spread it out to the people like PB & J

sandwiches or government cheese, they still want me to say please,

say please with a trick up the sleeve, no tricks for silly rabbits,

You see your chance then grab it,

They told me I only have one chance, then I took more chances,

Mastermind my time to rewind or fast forward to my destination,

Patience for a king, more patience when they sing,

But there's more money when you enter the ring,

Ding, ding, ding,

PERSEVERANCE

80's baby 90's raised me 2000's made me crazy,

They tried to Y2K me, but that didn't faze me, none of this makes me,

Day breaks mistakes and sunshine on minds,

Everyday feels like rewind, looking forward to the future from behind,

No excuses for giving up, only excuse was getting up,

Money could leave you stuck, thinking only from one position,

Moving in multiple positions, keeping the rotation going,

Practice makes perfect and everything is perfectly working,

Can't stop, won't stop, until I pop, popcorn with my movie, I can't let

Them move me, if this was the 70's everything would be groovy,

Peace and love keep me going, knowledge keeps me knowing,

Time fly's, time lies, when you do what you love,

Fly like a dove, do the impossible

When you are done make them ask who's responsible,

Set the bar high, everyone, reaching for the top shelf,

Take more and give more, life lessons walking threw the right door,

Create more, have more, don't live sore, move to Singapore,

Came a long way from nowhere, trying to get somewhere,

Have no care, no fear, but be aware.

IMMACULATE

Stylish demeanor made for a misdemeanor, just trying to get cleaner,

Wanted to look like me, but they said its wrong to look like me,

Now I'm thinking what can I be, also thinking what do you see,

Please let's not get to deep, we don't want to wake the sheep,

Let's take a leap of faith into the beauty,

Beautiful faces under ugly mask, every day is Halloween,

If you listen closely you can hear the screams,

Kings and queens never dressed for the part, so what is their part,

What's in your heart, smiles, styles, or hate,

No time to hate when you have time to create, or take a swim in a lake,

So much distinguished impeccable immaculate style in my grace,

Started off humble now it's in your face,

Exquisite beautifulness suffocating minds from knowledge,

This is brains and beauty, but no baby geniuses,

Predicting future forecast calls for more of the same,

Everyone try's to look the same, while playing a different game,

Take your time use your mind wisdom is a style too,

Told you again because I thought you knew,

New is new, don't be fooled.

INGENUITY

Injuries from industry moving forward, building worlds,

Destroying communities, new technology for old inventions,

This is a intervention on the mindset of the people,

Take a look into my pupils, tell me what's serious, no process,

No progress, big problems,

Then eureka, ideas blast off like speakers,

Ideas knowledge and execution recipe for ingenuity,

No perpetuity for the unprepared, one small step for man,

Trying to reach the moon, eating cheeseburgers with spoons,

Imagine the unimagine to create something amazing ,

When you get off the road they will say you were trailblazing,

They will never admit their failure,

But your failure plus their failure equals no failure,

Excuse were all sailors, lost at sea,

Seeking the land of opportunity, where all dreams prosper,

A million and 1 times, just to get it right one time,

We create what we make at high stakes,

Did it all for a potato and a steak,

Engineering God architecture for the sake of the test.

INSPIRATION

Sun rise sun fall, most appreciated when there no sun at all,

All the worlds knowledge moving faster than the speed of light,

Wifi on my mind, trying to shine on my decline,

No rewind, stretch me out around the world twice,

When it's good do it twice or do it for life,

Moving forward, looking backwards, got inspired threw the practice,

Young people screaming out no more plastic,

Social conscience with no conscience, wondering what's the mantra,

Grown up babies with a genius in their pocket,

We came to far now nothing can stop it,

Popcorn sat back watch it, notepads pencils plot it,

Young Frankenstein, who created this monster, game mastered,

It was fun while it lasted, new vision, on a new mission,

For a new horizon that looks foreign,

Good morning, new morning, old morning so boring,

Undiscovered what you might discover today, undiscovered what

You might discover if you pray, little kids play, old people say,

What a beautiful day.

<u>POWER</u>

Reaching 10,000 degrees trying to scratch the surface of the sun,

100 watts of power in my heartbeat, no defeat,

Can bring me to my feet,

Hovering then teleporting to new dimensions,

The power is never mentioned, pay attention, pay for friction, then pay

Uncle Sam, told him I don't want no red white and blue eggs N ham,

He couldn't understand, just a man with a plan,

1 thought changes the world, boys and girls creating new worlds,

Creativity creating everything,

Completing two tasks at once, with one thought, two tries,

No goodbyes, watching birds fly, as I fly in a plane,

Millions of thoughts flying threw a brain, how much power does it take

To create something great, not much equals good luck,

Don't get stuck trying to buck, the system, power to the people,

But where is the power coming from,

Came up with a formula to reach the sun, then started over just for fun,

Powered up, then exploded with the recharge,

Unintentional discharge, for my disregard

For how powerful power can be, now I can see, this power humbles me.

MOTIVATION

Standing ovation for this inspiration, on your knees praying for your

Salvation, patience and determination, gave me all this motivation,

No more waiting, we made it to a better place,

You can see I'm grateful in my face,

When we fail we keep going, when we win we start thinking,

Think to much we start shrinking,

No blinking, it happened all in the blink of an eye,

Some live, some die, ask why, you decide if you're living right,

Just remember you can die tonight,

Eyesight getting blurry, beauty is in the sight of the beholder,

Thinking about the future, thinking about getting older,

Lost solders coming home,

Thought you had it right, but you were wrong,

Stayed up all night listening to the same song, so wrong, so long,

Took the long way home, but it was well worth it,

Efforts to do better as light as a feather, the pursuit of happiness,

Bad days, make good days recognizable,

Contemplating on vacation, white sand and blue skies,

Did it all just to see a new moon rise, all lies.

DETERMINATION

Determination, emancipation, try to reach freedom,

Never quit, never submit, reaching your goals,

What unfolds, life gets bold, so many untold, what gets sold,

So many years old, just to get better,

What could be better, started to fly like we have feathers,

Can't stop, won't stop, until you make it to the top,

Outrageous tenacity consumes me gladly,

Better days in the wake of new dreams realized,

Ambition is my mission, it all feeds my vision, changes my position,

It gets hot in this kitchen, you talk a lot, but you should listen,

Up and down like car pistons, just trying to make distance,

From me and my opponent,

Different components, gives me momentum, gives me the wisdom,

To get where I'm going,

This is a marathon, I will not stop, only goal is the finish line,

Trying to push the line of what is possible,

Determination can help you reach the impossible,

Don't be fooled, don't skip school,

Get every lesson, to reach your blessing.

ACCOUNTABLE

Ask why, why lie, while doves fly, while we try to get by,

Look into my eyes, tell me is this sincere or no cares,

No fears, if you dare,

Who is responsible for all of these responsibilities,

Accountability in my accounts,

When in doubt, have no doubt, just keep going, always knowing,

There's only one captain of this ship,

Rare friendships, members only membership,

You did this, I made this,

Who can stop this, no one in sight, went from dark to the light,

Day to the night, life's a fight,

You have to wait for the right time to strike,

Timing is right, to take a bite out of life, only one life to live,

This is the right to live,

Understood this since kids, eyelids close, dreaming new dreams,

Waking up coming up with new strategy,

Do what you have to do, then wonder why the world mad at me,

They realized it was only me, won't let the discredit me,

I don't need no credit, I did this.

<u>DEDICATION</u>

One time, one dime, can make you want more,

Thinking five steps ahead, this is not a game of chess,

Ambition to be the best,

Wanting more and taking less, take what you can get, but get more,

Dedicated anticipation, no more waiting,

Life dedicated to dedication, made a better life,

Took a long time just to get things right,

Did it once, then did it twice, by the third time this was life,

It cuts deep like a knife,

Nothing can stop a mind made up, by the time you look up,

Some will give up, let the weak give up,

In 7 days made a week when you gave up, on the 8 day you got up,

Did what they won't do, now do what they can't do,

Practice made it easy, life is not easy,

One more reason to keep trying, no more reason for liars to keep lying,

No more dying, no more buying what they buying,

What's different when making a difference,

Understand what you fear, until fear can't understand you,

Make fear appalled you, then make it give more to you, who are you?

MOMENTUM

At God speed, moving in grace, taking a moment, screaming God great,

Wind in the wings of creatures at heights unseen,

You take your time then tell me what you believe, moving fast,

Then moving faster than a speeding bullet,

Take your time and get nowhere fast, take your time try to make it last,

Broke into a million pieces like it was made of glass,

Keep it all together, and then keep it moving,

Get left behind for not choosing, start snoozing, start losing,

The crowd was first with you, then they started booing,

It doesn't take much to get you going,

You know what you know until you know nothing,

Trying to make something,

Lead to making something out of nothing, confronting, then comfort,

This is real world results, losing grip on reality,

Tragedy and strategy, moving at unknown speeds, Leaves on trees,

Changing colors, please slow down, sounds like please go down,

I never listen, I never mention,

Just Breeze by whistling, to past that, you got to past back,

Around the world twice, or at least once in one life.

AMBITION

No more lost souls with no goals, no more babies crying and dying from
hunger, not knowing where you going,

Still moving forward, swimming in murky water,

Mastermind for the blind,

Plans written in DNA ,

Ambition keeps me wishing, premonition, a lot of food for thought,

No dishes, just keep going and going, infinity miles got me here,

No, I'm not stopping here,

I have more to do, dreams come true, in abundance,

Like your favorite show, try not to miss it,

I get it, you get it, but who did it, they say live with it,

No more cold days and dark skies,

Only clear skies and sunshine on my mind,

Only taking steps in the right direction, no more half stepping,

Another day, another improvement, another thing broken,

Pick your poison, building different immunity to poisons,

Nothing can stop me, even if it stops me,

Remember keep going and going, intelligence keeps me knowing,

Ambition is mines.

ELEVATE

Attitude fueling your altitude, what's your destination,

Loosing ground, loosing my patience,

Grass greener on the other side, until you get to the other side,

This is where I reside, until I dry up and die,

See the future in my eyes, two I' s in my name,

What's your game, what's your name,

There is no blame, there is no fame, until you make it,

Made it to the next level,

Understand life is no game, but what comes closer to being the same,

Eagles and pigeons never sharing the same airspace,

What's in your face, travel at your pace,

Anticipation and determination made me leap,

Starting flying, but who knew,

Skies was blue, when I aimed for it, make it this far up,

There's no turning back, until you get back,

Elevated mind body and soul, this was never the goal,

Living life, or getting old,

Wisdom getting sold, who's the highest bidder,

Gave everything you have, are you the winner or the sinner.

WARRIOR

Fighting hard, then fighting harder, so many obstacles in my way,

Million to one, taking on all odds,

Good vs bad, this is for eternity, no more certainty,

Time to fight again, time to fight more, fight against what's wrong,

Do you believe, or do you have faith,

Multi-task, until every task is master, education makes masters,

With time it can all fall apart like plaster,

Preserve your art, no one can stop what's meant for you,

Create one, then create another one,

Going from failure to failure, thanking Winston,

Stronger to speak then to listen, smarter to listen then to speak,

Might just make it if you stay on your feet,

Stay on your toes, nobody knows how the wind might blow,

Warrior or meteorologist,

Sacrifice 26 years of your life in prison, understand what's the mission,

Over stand all your visions,

Never afraid to change your position, make moves all around the world,

End up on different planets, manage, all savage thoughts,

Moonlight shines bright on a warrior soul.

GLADIATOR

Standup volunteer, scream out, throw me into the arena of life,

Hit the ground running, taking on all lion, tigers, and bears,

With no fears, looking the beast in its eyes,

For one second, not both, but one wonders who dies,

Who lies to live, and does it matter who has more to give,

One second past, and none of it evens matters,

Climbing ladders, with no plans for being at the top, will I stop, never,

Never was practical or conventional,

I listen for a long time and they never mentioned you,

When you are a winner, then they notice you,

Fame can consume you,

Take over your brain like vodou, now you doing things you wouldn't do,

No turning back, when you made it this far,

So far gone, hard to tell what's wrong, but we still sing the same song,

Falling on your back, but still making it back,

Making enough to give some back,

Never living in a life of lack, abundance giving me substance,

Taking from within to get the win,

Started with nothing, made something, now the whole world loves it.

UNBREAKABLE

Skin peels like orange peels, as Damascus steel wheels,

Forged in fire,

Breaking everything that lands in front of me,

Solidifying, putting it all back together,

Wondering what could be better, the truth, it makes me unstoppable,

Unbreakable, unbelievable,

Without the right formula this is unachievable, unreachable,

Like a water drop hitting a rock for a hundred years,

Will this get threw to you, or get to you, or into you, time will tell,

History,

Wondering is there any more time for my story,

Don't be fooled by using the wrong tools,

Learned that in school, strong foundation, long duration,

Bending the rules to the brink,

But never breaking them,

Saw more, then made more, step out your comfort zone,

Left alone, then became stronger,

I no longer, have time to think of weakness, only greatness,

In my heart, perfect place to start.

CONSCIOUSNESS

Think twice, think nice, before you let your mind speak,

Different levels, brings me to a different level,

Like getting past 6 feet with a shovel, and still ending up above you,

Prolific thoughts, give me more,

What I saw, could change a lifetime, change a timeline,

Change your mind,

What's more powerful then a mind made up,

What's weaker than a mind not used,

So many excuses, no more excuses, progress necessity of man,

Time to move forward,

Elevating the minds of men, eventually there are no more friends,

They hate how you think, maybe because you think,

Is common sense common, what's your comment, no comment,

So common,

It hurts my heart when I think, when people don't think,

Thinking more about tomorrow than yesterday,

Today is a good day,

Thinking greedy, more days like this, I wish,

Might just make it, if you stay conscious.

LIBERATE

Free your mind, free your body, free your soul,

Free your creativity, what's your goals,

If you don't know, then you should get to know, simple math,

Don't stray from your path.

Petty cash could blind us all, but we all know better,

Spend a lifetime trying to do better,

What a price to pay, watch what you say, strategizing all day,

Just to make away, dreaming of getting away,

Some say, someday,

Nightmares turn into dreams I never seen,

Chained and shackled, head to toe, still dreaming of being free,

Ambition screaming who could stop me,

Hearts taking over minds, how do you believe then,

Times up, never give up,

They will spoon feed you everything you need to know,

Feels like drinking out of a sippy cup,

Mud in eyes, but I still see,

Hate, hate, hate, have faith, love is the only way you can be,

Understanding of love could be the key to be free, reach for freedom.

CHAMPION

I am a winner, I am the winner, made it to another dinner,

No obstacle is unbeatable,

Was told its unreachable, then I reached it, then I touched it,

Then I grasped it, if you don't ask it,

Then you won't have it,

Nothing can stop me, try to stop me,

Most try and copy,

Do more, get more, results, live more,

Don't tell them what you saw, but explain in understanding what you

Saw, plans and ideas, coming from every direction,

Crossroads of life, keep going straight,

Never care who hates, they never can relate,

They want you to anticipate, in the end they will call you great,

Still wishing, still fishing,

Accomplish more than you thought,

Had more thoughts then you bought, all sorts,

Strategies, what a tragedy, if you don't have one, have one,

Make one, or have none, get some,

Then make another one, losing was never an option.

DEMONSTRATE

Explain your pain, make your gain, what's in your brain,

Things will never be the same,

Spread knowledge, knowledge spread, making the world a better place,

Wisdom explained, step by step process,

No process, no progress,

Made it known, then got gone, so long

Never felt wrong, but always sang the same song,

Always felt like someone could relate,

Dream chasing, just to be great,

Can't stop, won't stop, until you get it,

What's the code, going the road, worth more than gold,

Never stop trying to understand,

As I think, I make you think, small minds can make you shrink,

Inspire and motivate, the world is my canvas,

May these words paint a picture,

They say you can get a thousand words out of one picture,

Do you listen, or do you mention,

Carving out paths for future generations,

The more knowledge passed on, the less gentrification.

ACCOMPLISH

Perspective of a king, call it history, or is it his story,

Do what they say can't be done,

Fascinated with the untold, as the future unfolds,

New goals reach my soul, new scenery, they can't be me,

They can't see me,

Evolution of life, is there an evolution for one man's life,

What's your vision, what's your mission,

Don't let your dream go missing,

Impossible becoming possible, intended intentions,

Takes a plan to execute,

Understand then make a plan, or make plan to understand,

Tell me what can't be accomplished,

I will tell you what can,

In the past, it came to past, ended up last, then came in first,

Eventually you'll get the point,

There is no point, but we keep going, made it to the top,

Even if my lungs pop, clock stops, nonstop,

Even I stop, my goals will never stop,

I'm out for love to represent me.

MILLIONS

10 million, 20 million, 30 million more, these are numbers that I never saw,

Knowing I could do more,

Help more people, helping more people,

How do you contribute to others, contributing to the world,

There is no limit,

What's in your spirit, took more than one time to get with it,

This is how I did it, how I lived it,

Inspiring and motivating millions of hearts and minds,

Came to this earth pre-package, open up your package, let your mind

Manage, the seed is in you,

The seed can never leave you, you can reach millions when necessary,

Tell me what's necessary,

Reaching infinity, one to infinity, numbers became to common,

It was easy as 1,2,3, made it to 100,

Still going, numbers on my side, when on the wrong side,

Do or die, you can see it all in your eyes,

Men lie, women lie, you know the rest, what's left,

Time to confess.

MILLIONAIRE

Living life only in abundance, no more scarcity, hate me,

But now they all care for me,

How many times is to many times, was told to stop after the first time,

Now I get more time then numbers on a clock,

Some wonder when will I stop, never,

Got better, demanding success,

Results of being the best, never taking a rest, some say more,

I say less,

238 trillion, started with one million,

Knew I couldn't stop after a billion, never could reach the ceiling,

Now everything appealing,

But I know better, so I do better, what could be better,

Amounts unknown, same amounts got me known,

Started with no dollars, made it with only common sense,

They say it makes no sense, I say that's just your two cents, turning

Pennies into nickels, nickels into dollars,

I still remember when I learned the value of a dollar,

The lesson was valuable because I didn't have dollar, now I over stand,

Every dollar I count, the amount, not important.

ETERNITY

Living life fast enough to catch up with eternity,

Moving slow enough to feel like a eternity,

No sorority or fraternity, but we all play our part, where's your heart,

Lost trying to get fine,

Heard threw the grape vines, time is money, don't believe those lies,

Only once I died,

Living now with a better vision, they can't understand my vision,

They don't believe my mission,

Made it to my destination, the journey took forever,

But however, I love it,

Life got me spiraling out of control, let's keep the world spinning,

No answers, for when you winning,

Do it again, make it a trend, nothing last forever,

Greatest gift I have is time, so that's what I give, try to give more,

I do more, good deeds are never forgotten,

It could take a lifetime to fix a mind that's rotten,

Another nevruary came and gone,

They say never say never, but that never made sense,

Live life full off coincidences, don't be a coincidence, premeditation.

PERSISTENCE

I persist, I persist, I persist,

There's no never mind if you don't understand this,

What goes around comes around, keep coming back, moving backward,

To move forward,

I explode between a hard place and a rock,

Spread out threw out the world, discover me later,

No gas in the generator, still working,

Still hurting, this is life,

Made it pass the finish line with no destination, where am I going,

No one knows, so I go, but nothing could stop me,

From good to great, no debate,

So many told me its to late, never listen to naysayers,

To move forward, get forward,

Moving at a pace that's unaccountable, tell me who's accountable,

Quitting and spitting,

All means the same thing to me, disrespect,

Look out for the disconnect, all we got to do is connect,

Get together, to get better, we got further,

We made it, we persist, we persist, we persist, finally destination.

OPPORTUNITY

In this life so many chances, life makes me want to take chances,

The future only gives us glances,

Hindsight is only 20 20,

That won't stop me from getting plenty,

Success is at arm reach, finding everything that I seek,

Trying more times than the earth spins around the sun, 365 times,

Made mines, what's mines, in due time,

Your time will come,

Never taking what is given, but always taking my shot,

When you can do better, you should do better,

Even with no shelter,

New skies, bring new eyes, watching birds fly,

Be inspired, pay it forward and inspire,

Fears turns into liars,

Life gives us opportunity to never expire, what is desire,

Made it threw fire,

Ready and prepared, no time for being scared,

Life will knock you off that pedestal,

Take your chance but don't be a fool, no time to look cool,

PREPARATION

Ambition made me do it, so I did it, be prepared to get it,

What is a unprepared life?

Lost and confused, so I refuse, practice makes perfect,

No practice makes control, something like a control freak, new week,

Trying to make it to a new century,

Please don't play with me,

Tricks are for kids, but these tricks made us kids act different,

Tell me what's the difference,

Did it once, did it twice, by the third time it was nice,

Even with no energy, say this is your life,

Greatness is only one step away, giving up was never a option,

Plan B was always backing plan A as the first option,

It's possible, I trained, my brain,

Wright is right, wrong been wrong, sad songs,

Don't sing, life brings what's hard,

This is what I was made for, made more,

This what I prepared for,

Can't stop, until you get it right, what is right,

From the sunshine to the night, never keep your dreams out of sight.

ABUNDANCE

I can't deny it, I am surrounded, life abundance is prevalent,

Nothing can stand next to it,

Only in it, I did it

I can finally see the invisible,

The unforeseeable, this makes me highly capable,

Highly dedicated, always duplicated,

Made this look easy, gift and a curse in one package,

Having to much can wreak havoc, but it brought me paradise,

Time for you to roll the dice,

You only get one life, don't look for more, actions of the poor,

This life was meant for many, or plenty,

How are you living if you have nothing, lets come together and make

something, had more chances then the earth spins around the sun,

Had fun, but the foundation was discipline,

Made it this far,

Can't turn back now, live your dreams,

Then dream another one,

If thoughts can turn into dreams,

Then both come in abundance, widen your circumference.

VISION

Without dreams or vision you could perish, you could vanish,

regurgitated information,

Made for you to salvage, information in my package,

Does damage, you manage,

Hate, love, anger, and happiness, emotions can't control me,

It was they who told me,

I say they with a capital T, because it was he and it was she,

Both mad they can't be me,

The hate makes them not able to see me,

The big picture is never seen by all,

Different eyeballs, different opinions, what's your opinion,

What's your vision, what's your mission?

Sight and intuition,

Endless destination, was never discourage, vision can give you courage,

Made it to a new day, gave me all my new ways,

Everything became different, all I did was shifted, nothings is different,

This request, for this quest, is the same,

What we became, your vision makes you different,

It was never meant to be the same.

ASPIRATION

Hopes and ambition, becoming reality, didn't do it for a salary,

What's in you, what's in me,

Breaking out of the shell, becoming the first,

Was it the chicken or the egg,

No more mediocrity curiosity, or apologies,

This is the consensus of my senses,

Can't stop, until I'm on top, of my game,

All that I want, all that I can, all became the same,

Merging lanes,

More pain, more gains, did it all for my last name,

Selfish reasons, changing season, that made room for the good ones,

If none,

Get some, don't run

Head up to the sun, spinal cord to the wind,

Came back for the win, same ingredients in your dinner,

Same ingredients that made a winner,

Trying to survive the winter,

Made it threw the summer, trying to make threw the decade,

Feeling like a new slave, no new ways, with aspirations of being free,

AMBIENCE

The nicer things in life surround me in abundance,

Garden of Eden birth me,

Roots of a oak tree, my ambience is dirt,

Made everything around me clean with one swipe, no hype,

A type, B type, guess I have no type,

Enjoy everything beautiful, somethings are mutual,

Some things are debatable,

Not acceptable, this scenery, it was meant for me,

Excuses is for the weak,

Not able to mustard up the strength to be where you want to be,

No slicker but became quicker,

With no liquor,

Made it to the destination, with no hesitation,

Took time to learn patience,

Paradise was at the end of the rainbow, mind of a leprechaun,

Looking for a pot of gold,

Time becomes old, life's scenario,

Where will you end up, will you ever give up, will your mind get stuck?

INTOXICATE

My presents is intoxicating, no more waiting, one whiff of this will clear

your sinuses, mind your businesses,

Toxic aroma, is aroma,

Until I smelt something beautiful,

Something beautiful, the smell was invisible,

Still trying to figure it out,

Struggling to make it to your last breath, try your best,

What is the meaning,

Tired of screaming, why are you scheming,

It was all God given,

In the world with his children, as the world keeps spinning,

Trying to make this earth a better place,

With every breath I take,

But its carbon, that I spit when I speak,

Standing on two feet, future looks bleak, watch the words you speak,

Even if you can't see, the fog is to thick,

So much pollution, what is the solution, use your mind,

Our kids need to see the sunshine.

REVITALIZE

I started at a new ending, new beginning, as I start again,

Never looked for a friend, instead I became a friend,

There's only one life,

Some have a thousand, be grateful for yours, start thinking more,

Made it all happen with a new thought,

I don't know what you thought, not a mind reader,

But I do read life, life stories, sounds like a familiar favorite book,

New life, brings new light,

Imagine, the imagination of a young mind that brings something bright,

Tell a young mind that it's bright,

Don't lose sight, be ready to fight, no time for might,

It was the mightiest that brought us here,

Survival of the fittest,

Hesitation won't bring restoration,

This life brings new resolution, new resurrection, it's a revolution,

Nothing can stop me now,

Mind made up, only destination is up,

Heard shots so I ducked, never giving up, never know, what's around

that corner, you never know what could happen, who's the captain.

INVIGORATE

I give strength to everything around me, give energy to everything

around me, this life gives me unlimited energy,

Looking for synergy,

More power, when more than one power, comes together,

Will it ever all come together,

Transformation, going from one to two,

Two to a million, million to a trillion,

What are we building,

Unknown consciousness, what is the consequence, what a coincidence,

We all made it, some didn't make it,

This creativity kills all negativity, only felling positivity,

Far away proximity,

New thoughts, new reality, dress casually,

Requirements for the environment, that you cry in,

We live in what we create,

Contemplate, already ate, what's on your plate,

To much, eyes bigger than your stomach,

Grow every day like compound cells under a microscope,

What are you growing, what are you showing?

INCLINATION

Small thoughts, becomes big ideas, small fears,

Becomes your greatest obstacle,

Natural tendency, or propensity, dictating your prosperity,

What is your density,

This is no conspiracy, but I can only give you 99% of me,

A step, became one step, just take it step by step,

It takes a long journey to see the big picture,

Seeing it piece by piece,

Turning all, into all, making it all good,

Move fast taking your time,

Only time can tell, we tell our own story, mainly for glory,

Sometimes for truth,

Extracted from the smallest amount, made something beautiful,

Something meaningful,

One small decision, snowball into a mountain,

The capacity in me, the capacity in you,

One humane soul, capacity unknown, what is inside of you,

What can you get out of you,

Took what was in my mind and brought that into existence.

NOURISHMENT

Substances necessary for growth, didn't take much for this creativity to

grow, something like your favorite bamboo tree,

just grew 90 feet in 5 weeks,

Needed water for five years, never was there a day no one cared,

Attention provided every drop needed,

Neglect rotted everything needed, pay attention,

Can't afford to pay attention,

Then pay it forward, no matter what move forward,

Give me every vitamin and supplement,

I need the nourishment,

No time for punishment, time for refurbishing,

Gave things a different purpose, repurposed, fix what is broken,

Act like it was never broken,

Made it to a new day, after I thought a new day wasn't possible,

I beat the impossible,

This life blessed me with the smallest amount,

The smallest seed bear the greatest amount of fruit, in this pursuit,

Happiness is the key,

Sometimes locks are locked, your mind is the key.

www.ingramcontent.com/pod-product-compliance
Lightning Source LLC
Chambersburg PA
CBHW030533220526
45463CB00007B/2815